The One Left Behind

MICHAEL MORRIS

WESTBOW
PRESS®
A DIVISION OF THOMAS NELSON
& ZONDERVAN

Copyright © 2017 Michael Morris.

All rights reserved. No part of this book may be used or reproduced by any means, graphic, electronic, or mechanical, including photocopying, recording, taping or by any information storage retrieval system without the written permission of the author except in the case of brief quotations embodied in critical articles and reviews.

This book is a work of non-fiction. Unless otherwise noted, the author and the publisher make no explicit guarantees as to the accuracy of the information contained in this book and in some cases, names of people and places have been altered to protect their privacy.

Scripture quotations marked NIV are taken from the Holy Bible, New International Version. NIV. Copyright 1973, 1978, 1984 by International Bible Society. Used by permission of Zondervan. All rights reserved.

Scripture quotations marked NKJV are taken from the New King James Version. Copyright 1982 by Thomas Nelson, Inc. Used by permission. All rights reserved.

Scripture quotations marked AMP are from The Amplified Bible, Old Testament copyright 1965, 1987 by the Zondervan Corporation. The Amplified Bible, New Testament copyright 1954, 1958, 1987 by The Lockman Foundation. Used by permission. All rights reserved.

WestBow Press books may be ordered through booksellers or by contacting:

WestBow Press
A Division of Thomas Nelson & Zondervan
1663 Liberty Drive
Bloomington, IN 47403
www.westbowpress.com
1 (866) 928-1240

Because of the dynamic nature of the Internet, any web addresses or links contained in this book may have changed since publication and may no longer be valid. The views expressed in this work are solely those of the author and do not necessarily reflect the views of the publisher, and the publisher hereby disclaims any responsibility for them.

Any people depicted in stock imagery provided by Thinkstock are models, and such images are being used for illustrative purposes only. Certain stock imagery © Thinkstock.

ISBN: 978-1-5127-8925-6 (sc)
ISBN: 978-1-5127-8926-3 (e)

Library of Congress Control Number: 2017908501

Print information available on the last page.

WestBow Press rev. date: 9/18/2017

Contents

Foreword vii

Part 1: The One Left Behind 1
    Again a Bride 2
    Walking in Faith, Living in Hope 2
    He Heals All Our Diseases 3
    Defeated at the Cross 3
    God's Infinite Capacity for Suffering 4
    God's Love as Strong as Death 5
    No Plan B 6
    As It Is in Heaven 6
    No "What Ifs" 8
    On Eagles' Wings 8
    A Door of Hope 10
    We the betrothed ones 11
    God Works All Things for the Good 12

Part 2: The One Who Went Ahead 17
    Why Wasn't I There? 17
    At Rest in His Love 18
    Let Her Go Now; She's Mine 20
    But Where Is She Now? God Is Not in Heaven 22

Part 3: And Now? 27
    Why! 27
    From Glory to Glory 28
    Either None of It's True or All of It 29
    A Death That Will Glorify God 30
    Breathe on Me, Breath of God 31

Part 4: And So … 35
    Even "Gooder" Than We Think 35
    Life and Life to the Full 36
    As it is in Heaven 39

Part 5: The Way We Were 41
    The First Time Ever I Saw Your Face 41
    Bible References 42

Foreword

My wife of forty-three years was more than enough, the love of my life, and my only real friend. She went on ahead, and now I'm the one left behind.

Charmaine had just been moved onto the home-care hospital bed. It was delivered that evening, and I'd left her to take some rest after several sleepless nights. The bed was empty when I came back downstairs in the early hours. When I returned from having looked for her in the kitchen, I saw her lying instead beside the bed. She had rested her head on her right arm. It was as though she'd made herself comfortable, thinking, *I'll just wait for Mike to come back.* My love's left arm offered no resistance beyond its own weight as I reached over and lifted it to wake her. It felt so heavy, and as I let go, it fell back to the floor with a thud that I felt as much as I heard. There was no sign whatsoever of the vivacious, outgoing, caring life where it always had been for the nearly fifty years I'd known her. This time there was no familiar waking from sleep. I knew then that she'd gone on ahead and that I was now the one left behind.

I met Charmaine on our first day at University. In the words of the song, "The first time ever I saw her face, I saw the sunrise in her eyes. The moon and the stars were her gifts to me." (See page 41.) Over the years we had each become for the other, while hardly knowing it, quite simply our reason to live. To paraphrase the scripture, but to retain the spirit of its meaning, in each other we lived and moved and had our being. I once quoted this from Boris Pasternak in a letter to Charmaine: "You came in with a chair, reached up to take my life, as from a shelf, and blew away the dust." This is the story of how I've come to continue to live without her. It's a testimony to how God's goodness is helping me do this with love and purpose, and that He's even Gooder than we think.

But it's not just about me. In most marriages, with few exceptions, as well as that of our own parents, one will go on ahead and one will be left behind. How, especially as a Christian, is one to handle that?

In a way, this is where the rubber hits the road. God, salvation, forgiveness, eternal life and everything else that goes with them are either all true—or all false. The choice is ours. But praise God, He does not leave me alone in making that almost daily choice. My heart wanted to believe, my mind wanted to understand, but my soul cried out, and still it gently weeps. All this can only be reconciled where there is that peace God gives that passes understanding. Fortunately, we are not required to understand it.

Someone with experience asked me, "Is it well with your soul?" This led me to the song, which put words to what the Lord wanted me first of all to know and to do.

Far be it from me to not believe,
even when my eyes can't see?
Through it all it is well
Through it all my eyes are on you
It is well with my soul.

Let go my soul and trust in Him
It is well with me.[1]

But it was not always well with me, nor with my soul. Sometimes, believe me, it was not well at all! There was work to be done, but here was a starting point.

Since then many more songs and Bible verses have followed, as the Lord brought them to mind. They firstly helped me see what actually happened that night. He then took me back to how well Charmaine and I had loved and had always remained faithful to our first love. Although we were far from knowing God at the time, He knew us and was for us even then. Before knowing why, we would often remark on how our love seemed to be so much bigger than what each of us contributed to it, as if there was still more love coming from beyond us both. I know now that it was God's unconditional love for each of us that He somehow added to our own. It was Jesus's love for His bride(s) to be that we felt in addition to our own love for each other. I believe marriage models our relationship with Jesus. As the Bishop of London put it at William's and Kate's wedding, "All marriages are royal marriages."

Much later, Jesus spoke so kindly but so firmly to me of Charmaine having become His bride. He then healed my heart in a kind of rebirth into life as I was later rebaptised in the Jordan, as I will recount later.

This is not about how to do it, how to cope, and not even about how to overcome the loss. It's not about how to answer questions

---

[1] "It Is Well," from Kristene DiMarco's album *Mighty*.
https://www.musixmatch.com/lyrics/Bethel-Music-feat-Kristene-DiMarco-2/It-Is-Well
https://www.youtube.com/watch?v=T0dIWJ4t4Jg

like, "Why?" to which there can never be a truly satisfactory answer. "Why?" may even be the wrong question. It's more about growing a relationship with God in ways that will not be possible in heaven. We are heaven-bound, to live on in eternity. There is a unique purpose for us being "bound" here on earth. There are things we can learn, choices we can make, and praise we can give under the pressure of earthly circumstances like these. They can only happen in this sliver of time between eternity past and eternity future.

I am persuaded that it's our choice to believe. It's made in faith despite, not because of, circumstances. This choice is at the heart of the "fullness of life" Jesus came here to give us.

I do get all the teaching on God not being the cause of sickness and untimely death. If we are in any doubt, then we can say with certainty that Jesus is perfect theology. He is "the same today, yesterday and forever" (Hebrews 8:28 NIV). All who came to Him were healed. Even the wind and waves obeyed His voice. However, I cannot afford *ever* to forget that we are in control, that we have the freedom of choice that Jesus died to defend. But He is in charge, and He is good *all* the time. Although the circumstances in which, "Jesus said this to indicate the kind of death by which Peter would glorify God" (John 21:19 NIV) are completely different, perhaps there really is a "death that will glorify God."

This does not lay claim to being a handbook. It's a personal testimony of God's goodness and kindness. It's more about "How?" than about "Why?" and certainly not, "Why me?" How does God demonstrate His goodness and kindness in the midst of circumstances, every aspect of which seem to deny His love? At times such as this, even our faith is challenged, perhaps as never before. It can grow and deepen as never before, but it is also at risk of being destroyed.

It's then that we need God to give us more of that power to grasp the size, the width, the length, the height, and especially the depth of His love. This is a testimony to how he is doing that for me, and I believe he wants to do so for us all in proportion only to our need. That, at the end of the day, is what Jesus paid for.

Part 1

THE ONE LEFT BEHIND

Part of the tragedy of being the one left behind is this. You get to know how the life of the one who went ahead finally came to an end; you get to know how he or she died—and he or she doesn't. All this person's hopes and fears, joys and trials, and happiness and sorrow of an entire lifetime—all are gone and over with right there and then. You get to see how it all turned out; you see which dreams your loved one realized and which dreams he or she will not—and he or she doesn't.

In a lifelong relationship of intimacy and trust, we had no secrets. When you've shared everything of the greatest and least significance with someone for nearly fifty years, the circumstances and timing of this person's death are a truly terrible knowledge. You are quite unable to share them with the one who died. It's perfectly illogical, but it's like harboring a most awful secret. Not sharing it with your loved one is almost like the worst betrayal of trust. It changes your life, as they say, but not all in a bad way—for God really is Gooder than we think!

Charmaine was diagnosed with bowel cancer some eight years before. This followed an emergency operation to prevent a ruptured bowel, and she narrowly avoided death from septicemia. The cancer later metastasized to her liver and to both lungs. She went through multiple surgeries, radiology, and various kinds of chemotherapy; side effects affecting her voice, eyes, and skin. Hospitalizations for associated infections followed over the years. One of the four lobes of her lungs was removed. Later, another lobe collapsed. It was reinflated, but then it collapsed again. The doctors had stopped giving odds or bandying numbers long ago. That she was still alive was already off their scale.

Again a Bride

Between then and her becoming a bride for the second time (which I'll explain later), we were on a journey with Jesus that was as peaceful as it appeared outwardly to be challenging. Through it all, our eyes really were on Him. He provided total assurance that all would be well, and even now I have to say that it is still so—most of the time.

Walking in Faith, Living in Hope

While many Bible verses smoothed the way, we walked on a platform of prayer from so many people. As we walked in faith, we lived in hope. God lavished upon us that supernatural hope described in Romans 5:5 (NIV): "And hope does not put us to shame, because God's love has been poured out into our hearts through the Holy Spirit, who has been given to us." These were not just words on the page. For us in our particular circumstances, they were living words. Romans 15:13 (NKJV) told us, *"Now* may the God of hope fill you with all joy and peace in believing, that you may abound in hope by the power of the Holy Spirit" (my emphasis). And He really did fill us with joy and peace. Hebrews 11:1 (NKJV) says, *"Now* faith is the *substance* of things hoped for, the *evidence* of things not seen" (my emphasis). We were nourished by that substance and convinced by that evidence. I would even put it like this, if I may, with conviction: "This stuff works."

These living words informed our mind-sets, our worldviews, and our daily experiences. They're summed up very powerfully in Steve Backlund's statement, which we often declared out loud together: "If you're not glistening with hope then you're believing a lie." Some may find this hard to swallow. Well, in our circumstances, it motivated us pretty well to seek out the devil's lies. *This is all going to end badly. You'll never make it. God doesn't really care. Did God really say ...?* We were taught, while in submission to God, to literally laugh at the devil's lies, and he fled from us.

He Heals All Our Diseases

"Praise the LORD, oh my soul, and forget not all his benefits—who forgives all your sins and heals all your diseases" (Psalm 103:3 NIV). If we believe that God forgives our sins, and that thereby we are saved, then we have no option but to believe the rest of the sentence that He also heals all our diseases. The gospel really is good news. It's said that healing is not the whole gospel, but the gospel is not whole without it. Total healing is what we pursued with all our might. We adored the testimonies of healing that are so plentiful nowadays. They inspired us. Young people coming to faith have a new norm that we didn't have. Our ceiling is their floor. Jesus is perfect theology. He only did what He saw the Father doing. He made nobody sick. Therefore, God never makes anybody sick—and never did. He healed everyone who came to Him. His intention is for everyone to be healed, as we pray for them. This we know from John 14:12 (NKJV): "He who believes in me will do as I have done."

Defeated at the Cross

We also know we are in control through the freedom and authority we've been given to make the choices we make. Nevertheless, God is in charge. He is sovereign. There is no contest between good and evil. It's not "may the best man win." The best has already won. It was an unfair fight—a foregone conclusion. As C. S. Lewis puts it, "The devil is a defeated enemy in just the way that Hitler was defeated when the Allies secured the Normandy beach-heads." Nevertheless, there was much to fight for before they reached the inevitable conclusion in Berlin.

Just so, Satan was defeated at the cross. As the Son of God, Jesus declared Himself quite rightly to be in this world, but not "of this world" (John 8:23 NIV). Satan, where he had no legal jurisdiction, instigated a conspiracy to have Jesus murdered; this therefore made his attempt illegal. Satan was guilty of unlawfully taking Jesus's life. He was thereby lawfully defeated, condemned, and sentenced.

The only power he has is through our agreement with his lies that we, in our ignorance, give him. Yet, we have much to fight for before reaching the inevitable conclusion that Jesus will return. It is then that Satan will be revealed as a small and powerless being. "Was he the one who …?"

God's Infinite Capacity for Suffering

This is a hard teaching. God allows nothing—nothing—to occur in heaven or on earth without His knowledge. The very hairs of our heads are all numbered. "Not even a sparrow falls/hops to the ground apart from the Father's will/care [for the Father is sovereign and has complete knowledge]." (Matthew 10:29–30 AMP).

Job did nothing wrong! It was not that he was "righteous in his own sight" or feared that his children might go wrong and thereby leave a "foothold for the enemy." Even in God's eyes there was "no one on earth like him." He was "blameless and upright" (Job 1:8, 2:3 NIV). God could have prevented what happened to him, but He voluntarily limited His ability to interfere through what Oswald Chambers refers to as "providential permission"—that is, God's "very well then; but ..." (Job 1:12, 2:6 NIV).

We know too from the famous Romans 8:28 (NIV) that "in all things God works for the good of those who love him, who have been called according to his purpose." I'm told that Greek scholars have looked into the meaning of this "all things" and have reached the conclusion that it means *all* things. This verse wouldn't be there were it not expected that some things would occur that were less than good and would need Him to work on them for the good of "those who love him, who have been called according to his purpose."

But what is the purpose to which those who love Him are called? This is not a catch question. The answer lies in the very next verse, Romans 8:29 (NIV): "For those God foreknew he also predestined to be conformed to the likeness of his Son." Might it be said that through this process of working "all things according to his purpose" that we are somehow conformed to the likeness of His Son?

In His goodness, and in His love, God sees all things, knows all things, and feels all things. I believe therefore that He has an infinite capacity for suffering.

God's Love as Strong as Death

This was summarized for us in another "hard" saying: "We look to God to change our circumstances, while He looks to circumstances to change our hearts." We discovered that in this period between sickness being discovered and it being healed, be it here on earth or in heaven, there are nutrients to be found. We discovered too that some of the awesome mystery in the verse from Song of Songs 8:6 (NIV), which tells us that God's love "is as strong as death" of His "jealousy unyielding as the grave."

I read in letters written in our pre-Christian early twenties that even then God revealed to us that only love and death are forever, albeit at that time we were thinking more of the love. Only now do I know this referred to God's own unconditional love that He gave us each for the other.

No Plan B

Each day we chose not to give our agreement, not in any way to the one who actually brought these circumstances about; we would not do so and thereby empower him. Insofar as we empower the one to whom we give our agreement, we had no plan B. Again, Jesus is perfect theology. He did only what He saw the Father doing. God the Father never made anybody sick so Jesus could come and demonstrate His love in healing them. There was plenty of sickness around already. So instead, we gave our agreement to God. In so doing, we empowered the one who would use these circumstances to draw us still closer to Himself and to reveal to us ever more of His true nature.

As It Is in Heaven

There can be no sickness in heaven, so it must be said that God is incapable of making us sick. God does not just express love; He *is* love. It's against His very nature not to love. Sickness is the work of the devil, and Jesus came to "destroy the devil's work" (1 John

3:8). Indeed, Jesus showed us how to pray that God's "will be done on earth [just] as it is [done] in heaven." That is our calling, an integral part of a Christian's job description.

Toward the "end", Charmaine took comfort in reaffirming that she had already received the greatest healing possible. Her soul had been redeemed, bought back, paid for, "crossed over from death to life" (John 5:24 NIV). She knew the certainty of being adopted as a daughter of the King and would live with Him the eternal life He had promised. She was content, in clear-eyed confidence, with however God would bring about this relatively lesser physical healing, either here on earth or "at home" in heaven.

If there was a miraculous healing on earth, she would get to see Jesus. If not, then she would still get to see Jesus. Either way, as the only way we could explain to our daughter and her husband, it was a real win-win. Charmaine desperately wanted to be totally healed and to live. She wanted her eldest grandson to take her to dinner in twenty year's time. But whichever way it would be, she wanted God to have the greater glory. I am here, the one left behind, to do what I can to "broker" at least as much of that greater glory as I can be trusted with, to see and witness at least some of it.

Charmaine never heard this song, but she would have adopted it wholeheartedly. It speaks so much of her. "Nothing's going to take your praise out of my mouth as long as I shall live. I will not die, I will live!"[2]

---

[2] "Lily's Song" from Kristene DiMarco's album *Mighty*.
http://www.songlyrics.com/kristene-dimarco/lily-s-song-praise-the-lord-live-lyrics/
https://www.youtube.com/watch?v=1kFEgMYJyZ0

No "What Ifs"

We may not witness it at the time, but seated as we are with Jesus "in the heavenly realms" (Ephesians 2:6 NIV), I believe it is impossible for nothing to happen in heaven when we pray. It has even been said, "Prayers for which we don't yet see answers are merely gaining interest." We contended constantly for Charmaine's healing to be manifest on earth as it had already been accomplished in heaven—as did our family, our church family, and many other Christians of renown. But this greater glory was always front and centre in our thoughts. For better or worse then, and only by grace, we never ever discussed the big "what ifs?"

The closest we came to a Plan B was a Plan A2, to bring forward a holiday to France with my daughter where she had grown up and where we had spent the happiest years of our lives. Instead of at some time in February, we decided to leave January 8. It was to be a precious time together, but before that we needed a miracle and some "industrial strength" prayer.

On Eagles' Wings

On January 2 and 3, there was an annual conference at All Nations Church in Leicester. It was always attended by Paul Mainwaring from Bethel Church in Redding California and five to six hundred people from the UK and Europe. Paul has a healing ministry specifically devoted to the healing of cancer. His aim is to partner with God in creating cancer-free zones. He'd even been given a special pair of boots with which he was commissioned to supernaturally crush the scourge of cancer.

No sooner had we arrived at the church that Friday morning, and Charmaine had sat down in the entrance foyer, than she felt a stabbing pain in her right leg like a trapped nerve? Quite suddenly she couldn't stand up. It later became clear it was a slipped disc brought on through loss of weight and muscle tone. We could have seen this as a wicked attack to deter us, but God gave us the grace to persevere. As I'll explain later, he turned it to her good. We borrowed a wheelchair and joined everyone else in worship of our Father God. We *knew* that we knew, despite these or any other circumstances, that He is good all the time. We would continue to worship Him for who He is, not just for what He could do for us. That, in the spirit realm, was terrorist violence against the powers that mounted the attack.

Earlier that morning a lady from our own church, Jubilee Leamington Spa, had received a prophetic picture while driving to the meeting. She saw in her mind's eye, in the Spirit, a picture of an eagle in flight. Between its wings, a person lay prostrate on its back, protected by its wings. As the eagle rose toward the sun, its wings spread wider and the person who had been lying there began to stand in joyful worship.

She had no idea of the meaning of this, nor who it was intended for, until she saw Charmaine. Then she "knew in her knower" that the picture was for her—what appeared at the time to prophesy healing. Paul prayed powerfully into this. Gently but firmly he placed his booted foot on Charmaine's foot, symbolically crushing the cancer in her body. Again, although not always with manifestly physical effect, we well knew that it's impossible for nothing to happen in heaven when we pray, seated as we are "with Jesus in the heavenly realms" (Ephesians 2:6 NIV). We continued to contend for it to become manifest on earth.

A Door of Hope

A few days earlier, I'd been taken to some verses from the book of Hosea that I hadn't noticed at all before. They suddenly seemed to assume a special significance. The written word in the Bible is a "living word" through which God communicates those scriptures that are of specific relevance to us individually for today. Although spoken over Israel more than two thousand five hundred years ago, these words captured my attention—for the now.

Hosea 2:14–15 says (NKJV), "I will allure her, and speak comfort to her will bring her into the wilderness and speak tenderly to her. There I will give her back her vineyards from there, and the Valley of Achor as a door of hope. She shall sing there as in the days of her youth, as in the day when she came up from the land of Egypt."

To "give her back her vineyards" spoke to me of the return of the wealth that was Charmaine's health. The "Valley of Achor" refers to a valley in Israel known as the Valley of Troubles, to exit from which there would be a door of hope. The words that "she will sing as in the days of her youth" speak for themselves. They speak both for that youthful time of life and of the "youth" of the time when Jesus first becomes real in one's life. "As in the day she came up out of Egypt."

This had special relevance to Charmaine as her family fled out of Egypt when Colonel Nasser closed the Suez Canal in 1956. Although without any possessions, they rejoiced to leave with their lives. It was like a signature of God on these verses, specifically for her. It spoke much more to us of the time that together we "came up from the land of Egypt," out of a land without real hope, into which we had been physically birthed (see Hosea 2:1–3 NIV) and into the Kingdom of Hope into which we were spiritually born again. We had experienced the "joy of our salvation" (Psalm 51:12 NIV) coming to know Jesus for the first time for who He really is, the Creator of all things and the "Lover of my soul" (Hillsong).

We the betrothed ones

Although I didn't really pay attention at the time, Hosea 2:16, 19–20 (NIV) goes on to say, "In that day, declares the Lord, you will call me 'my husband' you will no longer call me 'my master.' ... I will betroth you to me forever; I will betroth you in righteousness and justice, in love and compassion. I will betroth you in faithfulness, and you will know [*yada* in Hebrew—as Adam knew Eve, as a husband knows his wife] the Lord." These verses gained greatly in significance in the coming days and weeks, as the Lord spoke tenderly to me in my turn of Jesus coming back for His bride—as He was to return for Charmaine in just a few days' time.

On the second day of the conference, Paul's wife Sue asked if Charmaine would like to receive more prayer. But of course, we didn't know that she had in mind that *everyone* there would pray. I felt moved to read out these verses 14 and 15 from Hosea—"then you will sing as in the days of your youth." Half of the five to six hundred people there were asked to worship the Lord, the other half to pray loudly and earnestly for Charmaine and I. This went on for a full for ten to fifteen minutes. Accompanied by the worship team, there was a glorious outpouring of praise and declarations of healing and wholeness. They had never done this before, but it was the industrial strength prayer we had come for. It was beyond all that we could have asked for or imagined.

How wonderful it would have been to end the conference with the kind of total miraculous, life-saving healing we hear about so often. We didn't really know at the time, but instead God had a greater glory even than this in mind. "I carried you on eagles' wings and brought you to myself" (Exodus 19:4 NIV), and so He did three days later.

Here is the painting that the lady from our church painted afterwards of her prophecy for Charmaine, just as she saw it.

God Works All Things for the Good

God had always used the medical profession to minister very successfully to Charmaine. Quite unusually, we had not gone for medical treatment for the trapped nerve, not wanting to miss any of the conference, but when we got home on the Sunday, the out-of-hours doctor prescribed some oral painkillers. They had little to no effect. On the Monday, our family doctor wanted to be sure that before leaving on Wednesday, January 7 (I'll describe the significance of this date a little later), the pain was not being caused by cancer having spread to the spine. He sent Charmaine for an X-ray.

Sadly, the trauma of maneuvering to take the X-ray caused more damage to a disc and brought on a crisis that left her in too much pain even to move. The doctor prescribed oral morphine or oromorph. I am going somewhere with this turn of events. The following day a hospital bed was ordered for home use downstairs, since Charmaine could not be moved until the oromorph had taken effect.

The X-ray came through with a green light—no cancer in the bones. Hallelujah! But clearly, we would not be leaving on Thursday, January 8. Our GP was determined to do whatever he could to ensure our special time together by controlling the back pain. We began to plan our departure for Saturday instead.

Wednesday, January 7, Charmaine's last full day here, was packed with activity. Saran, my daughter, came over from Leicester. Instead of her flying out to join us on the Saturday, we would drive together that day to France. We had always neglected to draw up a will. In touch with them over another matter, our solicitors had suggested we do this on the day before we were due to leave. As it happened, Charmaine was not well enough to go to their offices, so they came over to the house instead for us to sign and for them to witness the wills. Some would see chance at work here, where I would later see God's perfect timing. When asked the day before if we wanted to be buried or cremated, I opted for the latter because that's what everyone seems to do nowadays. Charmaine and I had never actually discussed it.

However, thinking that cremation was some standard and irrelevant wording when she saw it in writing, she took exception when it came to sign. "I'm not going up in a puff of smoke!" she proclaimed. "Anyway, I'm not planning on dying any time soon!" she declared with panache, and she meant it. The clause was deleted and initialed. Charmaine was truly stout hearted.

Things moved quickly that day, with the solicitors, doctors, health care workers, and my daughter's visits. We rearranged our travel and even located an International Red Cross ambulance service that would take us all the way there.

Just before New Year we had arranged for portable oxygen equipment to be delivered. It didn't rely on cylinders but extracted oxygen from the air. It was to sustain blood oxygen levels that went sharply down with any exertion, making it difficult for her to breathe. The two remaining lobes of the lungs, which had not been removed or collapsed, were being challenged.

Our operating mode over these past eight years was this. Whichever of the countless complications, side effects of cancer fatigue, or emergencies arose, of whatever kind, we would pray, deal with it, get over it, and carry on. Strange as it may seem to read about them here, they were all just more of the same kinds of challenges. We carried on regardless, fighting *from* victory, not *for* victory.

The hospital bed arrived late that Wednesday evening. The medical team to lift Charmaine safely into it finally arrived much later. It had been a grueling few days accompanied by several nights of lost sleep since arriving in Leicester on the Friday. Charmaine, while fully conscious, was a bit dozy because of the oromorph. I'd bought a device on Amazon that clips on the finger, like they have in hospitals, to measure the blood oxygen level and heart rate every couple of hours. I had noticed during the day that the oxygen level would go down and then recover but never to quite the same point as before. In retrospect, it became clear that what remained of her lungs were failing. But mysteriously, and quite miraculously, we were still kept from feeling any fear, let alone being gripped by it. And so, we finally said good night in the early hours of Thursday morning, January 8. I went upstairs to rest to keep going for Charmaine's recovery and our departure in a couple of days' time.

Somewhere in the back of my mind I had wondered, if ever there were lung failure, how would Charmaine get through the physical panic of not being able to breathe? The oromorph was brought in to deal with a strange and otherwise inexplicable "attack" at the very entrance to the church where we'd gone for a last-minute miracle. In the end, I believe it allowed a peaceful, if totally unexpected, pulmonary or cardiac arrest to occur without any distress. "In *all* things, God works for the good of those who love him and are called according to his purpose" (Romans 8:28 NIV).

How do I know that, and *what is His purpose?* Well, not without considerable soul-searching over the following days and weeks, as you can imagine. But the position in which I found her later that morning was totally without distress. It was of one who left the bed for some reason, disconnecting the oxygen in so doing. Then, having misjudged and fallen to the floor beside it, she placed her head comfortably on her folded right arm—just waiting for me to come back.

Never did we relent in our hope of miraculous healing. One of Charmaine's very last texts to friends and family read, "Mike's taking me away on holiday next week." Bless her. Nor did we languish in the despair of what if. We did not embrace death as God's will as a kind of victory over sickness, but neither did we cling desperately to life in this world to avoid defeat. Nevertheless, Charmaine knew no fear, and therefore the devil lost. The cancer was dead, but she is alive.

And again, the purpose to which we are called in Romans 8:29 (NIV): "For those God foreknew he also predestined to be conformed to the likeness of his Son."

Part 2
THE ONE WHO WENT AHEAD

Why Wasn't I There?

As I said earlier, part of the tragedy of being 'the one left behind" is this. We get to know how life ended for the one who went ahead—how in the end he or she died. At least part of the struggle is still loving Charmaine and not being able to tell her about that. It's rather like having the pain of a phantom amputated limb, only sometimes it feels more like half my entire body.

To know and to be known was such a precious gift that I hardly knew I had. There was not a single plan, ambition, or dream of mine of the past nearly fifty years that we had not shared together. Charmaine unfailingly validated them for me and somehow made them real before the event.

Now she's gone, and I hardly know where to put myself. What's the point of anything? I am having to learn a whole new way of doing life. It may seem melodramatic, if not trite, to say this, but two years on I'm coming to realise that my heart is broken. That's not to say I'm brokenhearted—that too, I suppose—but rather that my heart just doesn't seem to work anymore as it did. It's broken.

But God did not allow her to go and allow me to stay without there being a purpose behind being left behind, unique ways that can advance His Kingdom.

Meanwhile, pressing urgently on my mind was the need to understand what had happened that night. Why had Charmaine left the bed? Had she just fallen out of it? What was she thinking? What were her very last thoughts? Was she distressed? Was she afraid? Did she know she was going to die alone? Did she cry out for me? Did she cry out to Jesus? Why was I not there? What might have been our last words? Why did God not wake me? Why did she have to go at all? Why hadn't I prayed more? Why hadn't I fasted more? Why couldn't I fix it so it didn't happen? *Why wasn't I there?*

At Rest in His Love

A little later on, I had an intimation of what might have happened as God explained to me in increasing detail over subsequent weeks. I was struck by the well-known John 14:1–4 (NIV), which took on a perfect relevance.

Jesus tells us, "Do not let your hearts be troubled. You believe in God; believe also in me. My Father's house has many rooms; if that were not so, would I have told you that I am going there to prepare a place for you? And if I go and prepare a place for you, *I will come back and take you to be with me* that you also may *be where I am.*"

In a way I cannot explain, the Lord showed me that Charmaine got out of bed to be with Jesus. He had come back for her just as He'd promised He would. She saw Him coming to take her home to His Father's house as His bride—and got up to meet Him.

The One Left Behind

When the Lord took me to Martin Smith singing the Song of Solomon a few weeks later, then I knew for certain—Jesus had "come running" at last to claim His bride. He just couldn't wait any longer to take her with Him into eternity. In this context, it speaks for itself

> Do not hide me from Your presence
> Pull me from Your shadows, I need You
> Beauty wrap Your arms around me
> Sing Your song of kindness I need You

So it was that I found her—His arms having been wrapped around her. In Song of Songs 2:6 (NIV) it describes how, "His left arm is under my head, and his right arm embraces me." Just so, Charmaine's head was supported on the right side, as it were by Jesus's left arm, and it was as if she lay in the embrace of His right arm.

> All through the valleys
> Through the dark of night
> Here You come running to hold me till it's light[3]

Through the dark of night, Beauty had come to wrap His arms around her. If even I could see that, then she must have known it, and I was consoled in not being there. God is good, and He is kind—all the time.

In Song of Songs 2:10 (NIV) He showed me He'd said to Charmaine, "Arise my darling, my beautiful one, and come with me."

---

[3] "Song of Solomon," by Martin Smith.
http://www.songlyrics.com/martin-smith/song-of-solomon-lyrics/
https://video.search.yahoo.com/search/video?fr=mcafee&p=martin+smith+song+of+solomon#id=9&vid=b54bfd9ed8a92e4dc3ca59a6a5909a5e&action=click

I *knew* they had left together, arm in arm, bride and Groom, just before I got there. She was still warm behind the ear. What remained was the kindest way Jesus could have shown me His love for her, and for myself even though He'd taken her to be with Him. There was no distress, no striving, no despair in the way she lay, just perfectly at peace. She was "at rest in His love."

Let Her Go Now; She's Mine

It would be some months later in Israel, at the Jordan River, before he confirmed this again to me and released me in a way, that Charmaine had become fully His. Just standing idly in line, waiting to be rebaptised I "heard" very clearly, in my mind, "Let her go now; she's mine." Had it been my own thought, it would most likely have been something nice like, "It's all right now. You can let her go. She's with me." But it was said with such authority, and above all, with such love that it just could not have been my own thought. No, it was, "Let her go now she's mine!"

Only weeks later someone drew my attention to a verse I'd never noticed before in Isaiah 43:1 (NIV), "I have summoned you by name; you are mine," adding another piece to the revelation.

But before then a gradual revelation had taken place at a pace I could about deal with. The JesusCulture, Song of all Songs again evokes a glorious image of Jesus coming to claim His bride, paraphrasing 2:8, 11–12 (NIV)

Won't You dance with me,
Oh, Lover of my soul,
to the song of all songs?
With You, I will go
You are my Love You are my Fair One
The winter has passed and the springtime (the season of singing as in Hosea 2:14-15 (NIV) above) has come[4]

The "winter" of eight years of sickness had indeed passed, and for her the eternal springtime had indeed come. The Passion translation speaks of it in Song of Songs 2:10–12 (The Passion translation):

Arise my dearest.
Hurry, my darling.
Come along with me!
I have come as you have asked
To draw you to my heart and lead you out.
Now is the time my beautiful one.
The season has changed,
The bondage of your
Barren winter has ended,
And the season of hiding is over and gone.
The rains have soaked the earth
And left it bright with blossoming flowers.
The season for pruning vines has arrived.
I hear the cooing of doves in **our** land,
Filling the air with songs
To awaken you and guide you forth.

---

[4] Phil Tarver, "Dance with Me."
http://www.urbanlyrics.com/lyrics/phil-tarver/dancewithme.html
https://www.youtube.com/watch?v=sSbVGbQcLAQ

They had left together, hand in hand, bride and Groom, to the sound of doves in His/their land.

But Where Is She Now? God Is Not in Heaven

God knew I needed to *know*. He was teaching me that his "love is as strong as death, his jealousy demanding as the grave" in Song of Songs 8:6 (Jesus Culture) He revealed it me like this.

On March 22, 2015, I discovered a letter I'd written on that very day in 1972 that I hadn't seen since and had completely forgotten about. Charmaine had joined me at my family's home, my father's house in Manchester. Forty-three years ago, to the day, I had written a letter to the registrar of marriages in Manchester with a request for our wedding to take place there on her birthday, May 6. It was returned to me with a reply saying Charmaine had not been resident in Manchester for long enough, which is why I have the letter. In it I make mention of her having left her home on January 8, 1972, to come to Manchester. On that day, I brought her to my father's house as my bride to be.

Exactly forty-three years later to the day, January 8, 2015, Jesus came to bring her to His Father's house as His bride! In this letter, I have documentary "proof" of God's faithfulness to His word—to the very day(s)!

There are no coincidences in the Kingdom. I calculate that the odds of finding a letter on the day it was written forty-three years ago (making seven) naming the two identical and significant dates, are 133,000 to 1.

True to His promise, I know that Jesus came back to take Charmaine to His Father's house that she also may be where

He is. Indeed, she knew the place where she was going. She was twice a bride!

Sometimes I wonder to myself, *Where are you?* And again John 14:3 (NIV) affirms, "that you also may be where I am"—with Jesus. Like He said, she is "where I am." It's as simple as that.

Further, it says very clearly in Ephesians 2:5–6 (NIV) that when we were saved and "God made us alive with Christ … He raised us up with Christ and seated us with him in the heavenly realms in Christ Jesus." Where Charmaine is now is where we have *always* been, seated together in "heavenly realms with Christ Jesus." Even to some Christians this may seem a bit outrageous. But then, "Who am I to not believe (what is written) even when my eyes can't see."

But where are these heavenly realms? Generally speaking, most of us just think that God is in heaven. Everybody knows that. But then I recently heard it said that God is even bigger than that. "God is not in heaven; heaven is in God." Someone pointed out to me Isaiah 66:1 (NIV), "Heaven is my throne."

All during Charmaine's last summer, she had been reading the gospel of John with one of her prayer partners. They were struck by Jesus's references to His time not having come. Then, in the autumn, and especially her final weeks, she was impressed by John 12:23 (NIV), "The hour [the time] has come …" She identified all the verses that start to appear after that where Jesus said, "Ask and it will be given to you." It was the time to ask. And we asked, and asked, and continued to ask—that His name be glorified as she submitted to her small part in His "big picture," as she put it.

Returning later to these verses, I discovered a deeper meaning. I cannot say that Charmaine had picked it up, and we never discussed it. These are Jesus' words about Himself, but I think here as elsewhere, when revealed by the Holy Spirit, they can be justly applied to ourselves.

Verse 23 says, "The hour has come that the Son of Man be glorified." Had we not agreed that, whatever the outcome, God should have the most glory?

Verse 24 says, "Very truly I tell you, unless a grain of wheat falls to the ground and dies, it remains only a single seed. But if it dies, it produces many seeds."

Verse 26 says, "Whoever serves me must follow me, and where I am my servant also will be" in heaven with Him.

Verse 27 says, "Now my soul is troubled, and what shall I say? 'Father, save me from this hour?' No, it was for this reason I came to this hour. Father, glorify your name!"

Certainly, we were "troubled" by the advancing symptoms of weight loss, breathing difficulty, tiredness, and loss of appetite, even inability to eat sometimes and loss of mobility. But there was this powerful, overriding sense of there being a "purpose" for it all. Certainly, more people than we'll ever know received seeds that had been sown, of which they now have ownership, for them to water and for the Lord to make grow. I hope these pages will show how He did, and is, doing that—perhaps in your life too. Surely it was for this reason Charmaine came to this hour—for our Father to glorify His name.

Now, for some this may play contrary to teaching, "There is no theology of suffering because Jesus healed all who came to Him." He is our gold standard, that none of us has yet reached. Yet we know too that while we are in control—Jesus died to defend our "right" to make our own decisions. We are in control, but God is in charge of *everything*. "Not even a sparrow will fall (hop) to the ground apart from the will of your Father" (Matthew 10:29 NIV). Job did nothing wrong. Although "this far and no further" God did give Satan His permission. Later, of course, Job was restored, and with a double blessing. Jesus suffered and died but was raised from the dead. As Oswald Chambers suggests, might some such sacrificial actions be expected of us? He refers to it as "providential permission."

In those months or even years, between the diagnosis and the restoration of health, the healing—therein I believe lie spiritual nutrients we need to know how to be nourished by.

Part 3
AND NOW?

Why!

From receiving the news in mid-November of just three months to live, it was less than two. The family doctor arranged to call by very early that morning just to check how things were going. Even he was totally shocked.

Having dealt with the preliminaries of informing close family and the undertakers, reality began to break in hard upon me the following day, Friday. I began then, and continue to be thankful that Charmaine herself was not the one being left behind. I would in no way want her to go through what awaited me. I soon had to come to terms with referring to "I" and "me" instead of "us" and "we." Among many kindnesses someone later pointed out that I am never alone. It's never just "I." With the constant presence of the Holy Spirit, it's always "we," and even in conversation I haven't really worried about making that distinction ever since.

Having made all the funeral arrangements on the Friday, my daughter Saran and I flew out to France the following day on the flight she had always planned to take. God's timing is the signature of His presence and His kindness. Somehow, we arrived at our destination on time—although not quite as planned. How blessed in some ways that Charmaine's decline was so rapid. Saran came by on the Wednesday, and we'd been practicing our French for the Saturday departure. We went on to spend a unique and precious time together.

Nevertheless, I did begin to get ticked off with God. Looking out from our balcony across the glittering azure Bay of Villefranche (near Monaco, just outside Nice, where we'd lived for fifteen years) through the palm trees under a perfect blue sky, I began to ask, "Why could she not have lived just a few more weeks? Why could she not have shared this first and last opportunity to be here with our only daughter for the first, and if really necessary the last, time in nearly twenty years? Just look how eye-wateringly beautiful all this is! Why?"

From Glory to Glory

I don't know whether you've experienced this, but I've found that God has a way of speaking in such a way that you know it's Him. His voice is always full of wisdom, full to overflowing with love, but with the gentle and inescapable authority that not only persuades but also convinces. So here it came. "Would you … would you, Mike, compare what you're seeing now"—and you can see where this is going—"with what Charmaine can see now?" And that was it, my objections were toast, and it was suddenly OK in my heart. His words are accompanied by actions that we cannot achieve just by positive thinking. I came instantly to the conclusion too, perhaps on my own, that it wasn't any of God's fault we hadn't done this before …

As I "reverse engineered" the events of the past few weeks, I could see God's hand in them all. I thought of how it might have been: lingering between life and death, destroyed by bone or brain cancer; a husband caring for a wife in ways he never had to before; incarceration; agonising daily visits to the hospice; neither of us ever knowing if this would be the last good-bye. Instead "my holy one will not see decay." Charmaine passed "from glory to Glory," just as I had prayed so often but not with quite that end in mind. I rejoice in that even now. God was coaxing me, all but forcing me, to come into agreement with the wonder, the mercy, and the kindness of His ways.

The Lord allowed Charmaine to go ahead of me. However unwillingly, this allows me the freedom to do things we would not otherwise have done together. That is just a fact, and in it a question, "What are they?"

Either None of It's True or All of It

The moment you die is a very important time in your life, so to speak. This is also true of the person you spent most of it with. He or she gets to live on and reflect upon it. Did it go okay? Should it have gone differently, and what might we have done differently?

When you find that the person you know and love so dearly is so clearly no longer alive, when he or she always had been, somewhere in your mind you really begin to wonder, is all this about God really true? He or she just simply stopped existing? Tell me, is there really eternal life in some timeless place or is it just a big Nothing, as the lifeless Nada of a body lying before you seems to be?

What more might I have done had I not become so spiritually fatigued over the past eight years, and especially the past three to four years of Charmaine's and her mother's terminal illnesses? Her mother passed away less than nine months before.

Not that I didn't pray. I prayed just about every day, with Charmaine and on my own, but it could have been with so much more "violence!" I even gradually let go my weekly fast day in the middle of last year after many years.

Knowing what I know now, there's no way I can blame God. But knowing exactly what I know now, I have to consider very carefully my own part. I've heard it said that the hardest challenge of the Christian life is to navigate between blaming God on the one hand and one's own guilt and shame on the other, without foundering on either. As Charmaine used to say, "Either all of it's true, or none of it's true. There's no in between." As I've begun to describe here, all that is within me cries out, "I believe! It's all true!" and thankfully not just because I want it to be, but because it's confirmed by so many signs and wonders that impress themselves on my heart.

A Death That Will Glorify God

So dare I even suggest that God was preparing our hearts for the way in which He would glorify His name? My daily prayer was for Charmaine to go from glory to glory. I never meant it literally as some might say, "taken to glory," which is what God did. Although the circumstances are completely different, perhaps there really is "a death that will glorify God" (John 21:19 NIV).

But this kind of death, Charmaine's kind of death, is no defeat but a victory of childlike faith to wait on God as she did, ready to accept His best. What use is it to pray against that?

In 2008 Charmaine had received a word of knowledge for a "spot on the liver" (the exact same expression the medics used) from one of Bill Johnson's team members from Bethel Church, California.

That word was fulfilled through perfectly successful surgery. "But," she pointed out, "there was no 'word' for miraculous healing of the lungs." There was no personal revealed or Rhema word for all the rest. We simply stood on the general word that "By his wounds we are healed" and trusted in Him.

Breathe on Me, Breath of God

Apart from that, the only "word" we'd had was in mid-October 2014 when we spent five days at a Christian retreat in Wales called Ffald-y-Brenin. Quite without thinking, Charmaine heard herself say one evening, "Breathe on me, breath of God." Certainly, to have more of God's breath in her lungs would have been good. About that time, she made the only complaint I ever heard her make, which was, "I'm sick of being sick."

The next day one member of a prayer team there said, "The only thing I have for you is, 'Breathe on me breath of God,'" which was quite amazing really since Charmaine had not recounted the experience of the previous evening. Later, we did recount this "coincidence" to another member of staff there. When she got home that weekend, she found a CD still on her player from the week before had the song on it, "Breathe on me breath of God"—a third confirmation. What kind of a "coincidence" is that?

The first verses of the song are quite encouraging, as they speak of healing and restoration.

> Breathe on me breath of God
> Fill me with life anew
> That I may love
> What thou do'st love
> And do what thou would'st do

In retrospect, the last verse speaks prophetically more of heaven than of earth.

> So shall I never die
> But live with thee the perfect life
> Of thine eternity[5]

Some might actually see this, on the face of it, as a kind of deception, which is why it is so important to know God's character. The Israelites only knew "God's works." Moses "knew His ways." Ours too is to know His ways, His character, to know Him, to be assured of His goodness at all times.

Not to be flippant, I might even put it this way:

Rule 1: God is good all the time
Rule 2: If it appears sometimes that God is not good, see rule 1

Through it all, God was encouraging us in the present. At the same time, He gave prophecies for me to find later, hidden *for* me, not *from* me, to demonstrate that He really had been there all along.

The peace we had could be seen by some as simply denial on our part—"what will be will be." But God allowed Charmaine to go so peacefully, so relatively painlessly, as and when He did. I have little choice but to believe that He had been preparing our hearts for what was to come. I most certainly feel as though we had been prepared, both for Charmaine's part and for my own. Otherwise, by now, my life would be a wreck, just "rearranging the deck-chairs on the *Titanic*." Praise God it simply is not, even though at times it might seem that way.

---

[5] Edwin Hatch, "Breathe on Me, Breath of God."
http://www.hymnsite.com/lyrics/umh420.sht

In the end, and as the January 3 prayer at All Nations demonstrated, you can't pray successfully against God. His timing and His good and perfect will prevails. He may not be in control, since He has yielded that prerogative to us, but He is ultimately in charge.

I just can't imagine the God I know saying, "Sorry, buddy. Thank you for playing, but Charmaine's outta here." That's not the Father God I know.

Part 4

AND SO ...

Even "Gooder" Than We Think

By nature, I'm curious. I still want to understand God's ways. Why so soon? Why was Charmaine the same age as my mother and father when they too went ahead through cancer? Why now? If it was God's will, then what is the rest of that will for me? Mystery has its place, and we are not God to know everything. I love it that when Moses asked God what he should say to Pharaoh when asked "Who sent you?" "God said to Moses, 'I AM WHO I AM' Just tell him I AM has sent me to you" (Exodus 3:14 NIV).

I also believe that God wants to be known by us. "You will seek me and find me when you seek me with all your heart. I will be found by you." Jeremiah 29:13,14 (NIV.) God is not always nice, but he is *Good* all the time. He makes use of circumstances to draw our attention to His ways, to who he really is. "He who forms the mountains, who creates the wind, and *reveals His thoughts to man*—He who turns dawn to darkness and treads the heights of the earth - the Lord God Almighty is his name." Amos 4:13 (NIV.)

It has been said that, "we look to God to change our circumstances, while he looks to circumstances to change our hearts." Either He is in charge, or He is not, but He is even "Gooder" than we think. So, back to the user manual.

Life and Life to the Full

What does the Bible say? Where do you start? Some say that the Bible can be used to prove almost anything.

From a theological point of view, how do you answer questions about faith in this context? Is there more to know from a book that's supposed to have all the answers, or is it OK for it to remain a mystery? While some things must remain a mystery for our own good, otherwise we would already "know as we are known," I don't actually like mystery. I like to know, to have explanations for why things are as they are, who are we, why and where are we going. I still have these kids'-type questions.

Fortunately, God still speaks to us today, and He wants to throw light on at least a few of these mysteries so we can know Him better. Yes, He wants to be known. That's why Jesus came here to reveal the Father. "No one knows the Son except the Father, and those to whom the Son chooses to reveal him" (Matthew 11:27 NIV). And who is that, by the way? This is not exclusive. The answer is in the next verse, "Come to me *all* you who are weary and burdened and I will give you rest" (Matthew 11:28 NIV). Our only qualification is that at some point, we get to be weary and burdened. Anybody feeling left out?

He came also for us to have "life, and have it to the full" (John 10:10 NIV) and to model it for us. He went to the cross to underwrite that promise. He speaks through the Bible, through other people, through circumstances, and directly into our hearts through His Holy Spirit.

Of course, I don't have all the answers, but I have some to be going on with. I don't know where I'm going, but I know who I'm going with. I don't know what my future holds, but I know who holds my future. Also, I have that assurance of God's goodness and kindness even in the most trying of circumstances.

A few weeks before Charmaine's passing (I never refer to her "death" because she lives. It's the cancer that died), a thought came into my mind that my identity is not intimately tied to Charmaine. By that I think it meant that my identity, being found in Jesus, would not fail even without her. In fact, I think it has been strengthened as I've experienced so much of God's goodness.

Nevertheless, I am discovering afresh from experience that identity is also found in worldly things and human relationships. While I have been given financial and material provision in so many ways, relationally everything has changed over the past couple of years. My daughter, her family of four children under ten and her husband have moved to Canada and started a life over there. I moved away from my church family of seven years back to my hometown to be close to my brother, where I have no friends, and family relationships that must be rebuilt. As these relationships have been "stripped away" in the words of the song, what's left is almost entirely of Him, and so "I pursue Him", get closer, and hopefully prepare for "the more" that He has in store for me. Experience has shown me over the years, as we went from the known to the unknown that became known and then again to the unknown, "No eye has seen, no ear has heard, no mind has conceived what God has prepared for those who love him" (1 Corinthians 2:9 NIV). And since "God is love" (1 John 4:8 NIV), who can believe they are excluded?

I must now ensure that my motivation doesn't fail. Now there are no daily words of love and kindness, no touch in the night, no letters, no texts or e-mails, no future meeting date to look forward to, no more "see you soons" as so very often before. There's to be none of this before my departure from this world, which does have its newfound attractions. Where is the "Off" button?

But who am I not to follow through on what Charmaine had so faithfully endorsed, at what cost for so long, and as the Lord continues to lead?

While I feel so sad about it, I rejoice that Charmaine never did see her lifeless body as I did.

Thinking again that since the Lord, in His wisdom, chose for Charmaine to go home early, He must have something different/more for me to do than if she had remained. Oh, that He gives me the wisdom to know what that is, then the courage and the strength to do it.

I wanted *life* for her as her husband, her "champion" (as she often referred to me, her knight in shining armour who went out into life carrying her colours), and her lover. In a natural sense, I'm so disappointed not to have been able to give her more of that life! That was my mission as her husband, for Charmaine to have whatever she needed, whatever I could give her. I think it goes very deep.

Somehow the Lord had other plans. She has a new Husband. I submit to Him—and not without reluctance, I can tell you, but He is Good; He is God. All is not always well with my soul, but I tell it in the words of the song, "Let go my soul, and trust in Him."

When I think of all the operations, surgical interventions (tubes in the arm, into the aorta, under the skin, the vocal chords) treatments, hospital visits, doctors' visits, tablets of all kinds, body creams, eye creams, mouthwashes, oxygen, wheelchair, hospital bed at home—I am just totally in awe of Charmaine's faithful, unwavering dedication to the process. She often said she could not have done it without me, but although I hardly knew it, I drew my own strength from her inspired steadfastness. I long to tell her that.

As it is in Heaven

One day, when I see her again, I'll tell Charmaine that the strength she drew from me I in turn had drawn from her. We'll reminisce about our lives as if she had remained here with me. I can almost hear her say to me, when there I awake, "Hello, Mike. It's me, Charmaine…. You're home." Meanwhile I know that I've been "left behind" to fulfill a legacy, to join with others to bring Heaven to earth through prayer and obedience.

But, after the first 6 months of "euphoria" when everyone still grieves with you, I still had to get through the next 12 months. I've since learned that those 12 months that follow can be a critical part of the "grieving" process and of the strengthening – or in some cases the destruction - of faith. Strange as it may seem it was only much later that I would even associate the word "grieving" with what was happening. Words like "grieving" and "bereavement" had just never occurred to me. With hindsight that next period began as I was in Israel. It ended approximately 12 months later.

Charmaine and I had planned some months ahead to join a mission trip to Israel with a well-known church leader. People said I was very brave to go despite everything. Well, it didn't seem like being brave to me. However, when I got there and revisited some of our so favorite places and times, I began to realise the depths of the challenges. But God was intent as usual on turning all things to good.

Some will have heard of Canon Andrew White, otherwise known as the Vicar of Baghdad. Andrew was a Canon at Coventry Cathedral when we lived nearby, so we met on several occasions at talks he gave there. Shortly after my re-baptism in the Jordan we went up to Jerusalem. The Christchurch coffee-shop, just inside the Jaffa Gate, is a "watering hole" for anyone and everyone passing through. It's a place for Andrew to meet whoever may be visiting.

On one particular day he was sitting there, our eyes met and I had no option but to share very briefly the events of the past few months. If anyone has known a person who has ministered into even a fraction of the situations he has, they'll know something of the depths of their compassion. I can only say it was as close as I will ever be in this world to looking into the eyes of Jesus as I saw him feel my loss even as I did myself.

Twice I've mentioned his eyes, which then opened wide like those of an Old Testament prophet. In what seemed to be the voice of an Isaiah he prophesied over the rest of my life, "It begins here, and God will never let you down."

There then began to unfold a sequel to this book, which is still being written. If anything, it's an even more amazing testimony to God's goodness, but also to the ingenuity with which He manifests it in ways that are uniquely His – so you just know in your knower that God is even Gooder than we think.

Part 5
THE WAY WE WERE

The First Time Ever I Saw Your Face

The first time, ever I saw your face
I thought the sun rose in your eyes
And the moon and the stars
Were the gifts you gave

And the first time, ever I lay with you
I knew our joy
Would fill the earth, my love
And last, till the end of time

Roberta Flack, "The First Time"

http://www.azlyrics.com/
lyrics/robertaflack/thefirst
timeeverisawyourface.html

https://video.search.yahoo.com/search/video?fr=mcafee&p=roberta+flack+the+first+time#id=2&vid=7bea37a48c965fbef7ebf6667c956da8&action=view

Bible References

NIV: https://www.biblegateway.com/versions/New-International-Version-NIV-Bible/#copy Up to 500 verses without prior permission

NKJV: https://www.biblegateway.com/versions/New-King-James-Version-NKJV-Bible/#copy Up to 500 verses without prior permission

AMP: https://www.biblegateway.com/versions/New-King-James-Version-NKJV-Bible/#copy

Permission http://www.lockman.org/ http://www.lockman.org/tlf/copyright.php#amplified Up to 500 verses without prior permission

Printed in Great Britain
by Amazon